Grammy's Favorite
Knits for Baby

Doreen L. Marquart

Dedication

To my daughters-in-law: LeAnn, Katie, and Melissa. You are all such welcome additions to our family. I feel truly blessed to have each of you as my daughter! And to Addie, the first of hopefully many grandchildren whom I will have the joy and pleasure to knit for. I look forward to the day I can pass my love of knitting on to you!

Acknowledgments

I would like to thank:

My customers, who are first and foremost my friends. Thanks for allowing me to bounce my design ideas off of you. And thank you for always giving me your honest opinions, good or bad!

The yarn companies who continue to supply the wonderful yarns for designing and knitting. It's great to have such wonderful fibers to work with!

And Martingale & Company, for allowing me so much freedom in sharing my creative designs with the knitting world. Once again, it's been a pleasure to work with everyone.

Grammy's Favorite Knits for Baby
© 2011 by Doreen L. Marquart

Martingale®
& C O M P A N Y

Martingale & Company
19021 120th Ave. NE, Suite 102
Bothell, WA 98011 USA
www.martingale-pub.com

Printed in China
16 15 14 13 12 11   8 7 6 5 4 3 2 1

Library of Congress Cataloging-in-Publication Data is available upon request.

ISBN: 978-1-60468-030-0

MISSION STATEMENT

Dedicated to providing quality products and service to inspire creativity.

CREDITS

President & CEO ● Tom Wierzbicki

Editor in Chief ● Mary V. Green

Managing Editor ● Tina Cook

Developmental Editor ● Karen Costello Soltys

Technical Editor ● Ursula Reikes

Copy Editor ● Sheila Chapman Ryan

Design Director ● Stan Green

Production Manager ● Regina Girard

Illustrator ● Robin Strobel

Cover & Text Designer ● Regina Girard

Photographer ● Brent Kane

Contents

Introduction

Babies and knitting just seem to go hand in hand. Whenever I hear that someone is expecting a baby, I immediately go into "baby mode" and start planning what to knit for them. Over the years I've created my own patterns for baby gifts, and these designs have become my favorites and the ones I turn to when I need a gift for a little one. With the birth of my first granddaughter, Addison, my "baby mode" knitting really kicked in. Note the photo on the title page (taken by Addie's mom, LeAnn) is Addie on her first birthday wearing the cupcake hat that inspired this book to become a reality.

Knitting for little ones is so much fun, and the projects give instant gratification. In no time at all an entire ensemble can be constructed. You may even want to knit up a couple of ensembles to have on hand—one for a boy and one for a girl. Then you'll be prepared no matter what!

I'm pleased to share with you my tried-and-true baby and toddler patterns. This is a collection of my favorite designs, the ones that I have made over the years for gifts. They have withstood the test of time and are as stylish today as they were when my own boys were babies. They are basic, classic designs that are also fun to make. I hope you enjoy knitting them for the "small fry" in your life as much as I've enjoyed being able to share them with you.

Cupcake Cutie Cap

The perfect cap for your special "cupcake."
Change the color of the "frosting" and
it's adorable on a little boy too!

SKILL LEVEL

Intermediate ◖■■■▢

SIZES

Circumference: Approx 17½ (18½)" stretched,
12 (13)" unstretched

MATERIALS

Yarn: Dream Baby DK from Plymouth Yarn
Company Inc. (50% acrylic, 50% nylon;
50 g/1.75 oz; 183 yds/166 m) or equivalent
DK-weight yarn (❸)

A 1 skein in color 113 (brown); *OR* approx 90
yds for cake

B 1 skein in color 306 (pink); *OR* approx 60 yds
for frosting

Small amount of red DK-weight yarn for cherry
on top

Needles: Size 5 (3.75 mm) 16"-long circular and
double-pointed needles, or size to attain gauge

Notions: 1 stitch marker

GAUGE

5½ sts and 7½ rows = 1" in St st

CUPCAKE

Cake

Using 16"-long circular needle and A, CO 96 (104)
sts. Join, being careful not to twist sts, pm to
denote beg of rnd.

Work in K2, P2 ribbing until piece measures 2½"
from beg.

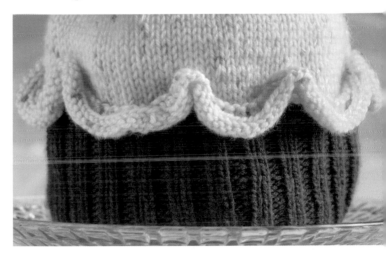

Frosting

Change to B. Knit 1 rnd. Purl 1 rnd.

Change to St st (knitting every rnd) and cont in St st
until piece measures a total of 6" from beg.

Crown

Work decs as follows, switching to dpns when
necessary.

Rnd 1: *K10 (11), K2tog; rep from * around.

Rnd 2: *K9 (10), K2tog; rep from * around.

Rnd 3: *K8 (9), K2tog; rep from * around.

Cont dec as est, knitting 1 less st between decs until 8 sts rem. Cut yarn, thread through rem sts, and secure tightly.

Ruffle

Use 16"-long circular needle and B. With RS facing you and holding cake (ribbing section) on top, PU 96 (104) sts around, going through loops of purl ridge closest to cake section. Pm to denote beg of rnd.

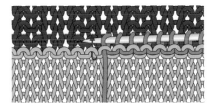

Rnd 1: Knit.

Rnd 2 (inc rnd): *K1, YO, rep from * around—192 (208) sts.

Rnds 3–6: Knit.

BO all sts purlwise.

FINISHING

Make small pom-pom for the cherry, approx 1" in diameter, out of red yarn, and attach firmly to top of hat. Weave in all ends.

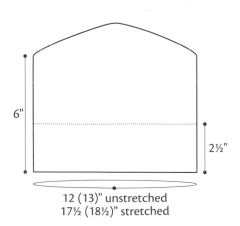

6"

2½"

12 (13)" unstretched
17½ (18½)" stretched

Pom-Pom

If you don't have a pom-pom maker, you can make one yourself by following these instructions. While pom-poms aren't my favorite thing to make, they are quite fast and easy.

1. Cut two circles from cardboard, 1½" in diameter. Cut a hole in the center of each circle about ¾" in diameter. Thread a long piece of yarn through a tapestry needle. Hold the two circles together, insert the needle into the hole, wrap it around, and then back through the hole. Repeat, working evenly around the circle, rethreading the needle when necessary until the circle is filled completely. When you think you have it full enough, add some more. The fuller, the better!

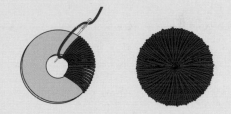

2. Use sharp scissors to cut the yarn around the edge between the two pieces of cardboard.

3. Cut a 12"-long piece of yarn. Run this yarn between the two cardboard circles and tie it very tightly. Slide the cardboard circles off the pom-pom. Fluff the pom-pom and trim any uneven ends.

Chevrons and Lace Blanket

What little one wouldn't want to cuddle up in a soft cozy blanket? This blanket is easy enough to make quickly, but has enough stitch design that you won't lose interest while knitting it.

SKILL LEVEL

Easy ◼◼◻◻

SIZE

Approx 34" x 40" when blocked

MATERIALS

Yarn: 6 skeins of Sport Weight from Claudia Hand Painted Yarns (100% merino wool; 100 g/3½ oz; 225 yds/200 m) in color Stormy Days; *OR* approx 1300 yds of equivalent sport-weight yarn (2)

Needles: Size 6 (4 mm) circular needle (29" or longer), or size to attain gauge

GAUGE

5½ sts and 8 rows = 1" in St st

1 pattern rep = 1¾" wide

CHEVRON LACE PATTERN

(Multiple of 10 sts plus 7 sts)

Rows 1, 3, 5, 7, 9, 11, and 13: K4, *YO, K3, sl 1-K2tog-psso, K3, YO, K1; rep from * across row to last 3 sts, K3.

Rows 2, 4, 6, 8, 10, and 12: K3, purl to last 3 sts, K3.

Rows 14–20: Knit.

Rep these 20 rows for patt.

BLANKET

CO 197 sts.

Knit 8 rows.

Beg chevron lace patt and cont until blanket measures approx 40", ending with row 19 of patt.

BO loosely knitwise on WS.

FINISHING

Weave in all ends. Block if desired.

Modular Cardigan and Star-Topped Hat

This cozy cardigan is perfect for either a boy or a girl. The boxy styling makes it extra comfy. Add a matching hat and your special little one is ready to go!!

SKILL LEVEL

Easy ●■□□

SIZES

To fit: Up to 6 (12, 18, 24) months

Finished chest measurement: 18 (20, 22, 24)"

Back length: 9 (10, 11, 12)"

Sleeve length: 6½ (7½, 8, 8½)"

Hat: 14 (15¼, 16½, 17¾)" in circumference

MATERIALS

Yarn: Meriboo from Frog Tree Yarns (70% merino wool, 30% bamboo; 50 g/1.75 oz; 105 yds/96 m); *OR* equivalent DK-weight yarn (3)

A 2 (2, 3, 3) skeins in color 93 (yellow); *OR* approx 185 (210, 240, 270) yds

B 1 (1, 2, 2) skeins in color 46 (green); *OR* approx 75 (95, 120, 145) yds

Needles: Size 4 (3.5 mm) and 5 (3.75 mm) circular needles (16" long for hat and 29" long for cardigan); size 5 (3.75) double-pointed needles for hat

Notions: 4 stitch markers, 4 stitch holders, 1 button—½" diameter

GAUGE

5½ sts and 7 rows = 1" in St st on size 5 needles

CARDIGAN

Yoke

Yoke is worked from the chest up to the neckband.

Using 29"-long size 4 circular needle and B, provisionally CO 190 (205, 220, 236) sts (see "Provisional Cast On" on page 56) as follows: CO 25 (27, 30, 32) sts for left front, pm, CO 45 (48, 50, 54) sts for sleeve, pm, CO 50 (55, 60, 64) sts for back, pm, CO 45 (48, 50, 54) sts for sleeve, pm, CO 25 (27, 30, 32) sts for right front.

Knit 1 row.

Striped yoke is made by knitting 2 rows (1 ridge) of A, then 2 rows of B throughout. Change to A and cont yoke as follows.

Row 1 (RS dec row): *Knit to 2 sts before marker, K2tog, sm, K2tog; rep from * 3 times, knit to end of row (8 sts dec).

Row 2: Knit.

Rep rows 1 and 2 until 62 (77, 84, 92) sts rem. Cut A.

Carrying Yarns

Since you are doing just two rows of each color at a time, it's not necessary to cut the yarn at each color change. Simply twist the yarns and carry them up along the side as you go.

Neck Band

With B, knit 3 rows. BO all sts on WS.

Divide for Body and Sleeves

With RS of yoke facing you, remove provisional CO, place first 25 (27, 30, 32) sts on st holder to be used later for left front, next 45 (48, 50, 54) sts on size 5 straight needle for sleeve, next 50 (55, 60, 64) sts on second st holder for back, next 45 (48, 50, 54) sts on third st holder for other sleeve, and last 25 (27, 30, 32) sts on fourth st holder for right front.

Sleeves

With RS facing you, using size 5 straight needles and A, work in St st and AT SAME TIME, dec 1 st at each end of seventh row and every following fourth row until 27 (30, 32, 34) sts rem; work decs as follows: K1, ssk, knit to last 3 sts, K2tog, K1.

Work even until sleeve measures 6 (7, 7½, 8)" or ½" less than desired finished length from bottom of yoke, ending with WS row.

Change to size 4 needles and B, knit 5 rows.

BO on WS. Work second sleeve in same manner.

Body

With RS facing you, return body sts to size 5 circular needle. Work in St st until piece measures 8½ (9½, 10½, 11½)" from top of shoulder, ending with WS row. Cut A.

Attach B and knit 5 rows.

BO all sts on WS.

Button Band

Row 1: With RS facing you, using size 4 straight needles and B, PU 38 (43, 48, 53) sts along edge of right front.

Rows 2–5: Knit.

BO all sts on WS.

Buttonhole Band

Row 1: With RS facing you, using size 4 straight needles and B, PU 38 (43, 48, 53) sts along edge of left front.

Row 2: Knit.

Row 3: Knit to last 3 sts, YO, K2tog, K1.

Rows 4 and 5: Knit.

BO all sts on WS.

Finishing

Sew sleeve underarm seams (see "Flat Seam Assembly" on page 59). Sew button to correspond with buttonhole. Weave in all ends.

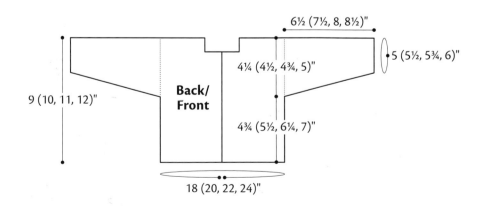

6½ (7½, 8, 8½)"

5 (5½, 5¾, 6)"

4¼ (4½, 4¾, 5)"

Back/ Front

9 (10, 11, 12)"

4¾ (5½, 6¼, 7)"

18 (20, 22, 24)"

STAR-TOPPED HAT

Beg at band, using 16"-long size 4 circular needle and B, CO 77 (84, 91, 98) sts. Join, being careful not to twist sts, pm to denote beg of rnd.

Border

Rnds 1, 3, 7, and 11: Knit with B.

Rnds 2, 4, and 8: Purl with B.

Rnds 5 and 9: Knit with A.

Rnds 6 and 10: Purl with A.

Rnd 12: Purl with B. Cut B.

Body

Change to size 5 circular needle, with A work in St st until hat measures 4 (4½, 4½, 5)" from beg.

Crown

Rnd 1 (dec rnd): K4 (4, 5, 5), ddc, *K8, (9, 10, 11), ddc; rep from * to last 4 (5, 5, 6) sts, K4 (5, 5, 6).

Rnd 2 and all even-numbered rnds: Knit.

Rnd 3 (dec rnd): K3 (3, 4, 4), ddc, *K6 (7, 8, 9), ddc; rep from * to last 3 (4, 4, 5) sts, K3 (4, 4, 5).

Cont dec as est, knitting 2 fewer sts between dec until 7 sts rem. Cut yarn, leaving approx 6" tail. Thread yarn through rem sts, pull tight, and secure.

Finishing

Weave in all ends. Block if desired.

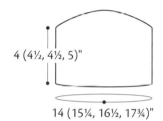

4 (4½, 4½, 5)"

14 (15¼, 16½, 17¾)"

Comfy Cozy Cardigan

Need a baby gift in a hurry? This is the perfect one. By making buttonholes on both bands as you go, you could have several of these sweaters made up ahead of time and simply attach buttons to the appropriate side after the baby is born!

SKILL LEVEL
Easy ◖■□□

SIZES
To fit: Up to 6 (12, 18, 24) months

Finished chest measurement: 18 (20, 22, 24)" when buttoned

Back length: 9½ (10½, 11½, 12½)"

Sleeve length: 6 (6½, 7½, 8½)"

MATERIALS
Yarn: 2 (2, 3, 3) skeins of Fortissima Socka Teddy from Schoeller-Stahl Yarns (65% nylon, 35% superwash wool; 50 g/1.75 oz; 137 yds/125 m) in color 6; *OR* approx 260 (295, 335, 380) yds of equivalent DK-weight yarn ⟨3⟩

Needles: Size 5 (3.75 mm) needles, or size to attain gauge

Notions: 6 stitch markers, 5 stitch holders, 5 buttons—½" diameter

GAUGE
5½ sts and 8 rows = 1" in St st

Cardigans— for a Boy or a Girl?
Since this sweater is knit in one piece with the buttonhole and button bands knit right on, it's important to remember to work buttonhole rows at appropriate measurements. Buttonhole rows have been written with buttonholes worked on both bands. That way you can make this sweater without knowing the sex of the baby and apply the buttons after he or she is born! If you know the sex, simply work buttonholes on the appropriate side (right for girls, left for boys) and omit them on the other side.

BORDER
Beg at lower edge, CO 106 (117, 128, 139) sts.

Rows 1–4: Knit, marking first row as RS.

Row 5 (buttonhole row): K3, YO, K2tog, knit to last 4 sts, YO, K2tog, K2.

Rows 6–9: Knit.

Row 10: (WS) K6, pm, P16 (19, 22, 25), pm, K12, pm, P38 (43, 48, 53), pm, K12, pm, P16 (19, 22, 25), pm, K6.

BODY

Row 1 (RS): Knit.

Row 2: K6, P16 (19, 22, 25), K12, P38 (43, 48, 53), K12, P16 (19, 22, 25), K6.

Rep last 2 rows until piece measures 5½ (6, 6½, 7)" from beg, ending with WS row, and AT SAME TIME work buttonhole row every 16 (18, 20, 22) rows. There will be 8 (9, 10, 11) ridges between buttonholes. (Note: When counting rows/ridges between buttonholes, do *not* count the 2 rows/ 1 ridge where buttonhole was worked.)

DIVIDE FOR FRONT AND BACK

On next row, K28 (31, 34, 37) and place sts on holder to be used later for right front, K50 (55, 60, 65) sts for back, place rem 28 (31, 34, 37) sts on second holder to be used later for left front.

BACK

Beg with WS row, cont working in St st while keeping first and last 6 sts in garter st until back measures 9½ (10½, 11½, 12½)" from beg, ending with WS row.

Divide sts onto 3 holders:

Holders 1 and 3: 15 (17, 19, 21) sts

Holder 2: 20 (21, 22, 23) sts

RIGHT FRONT

With WS facing you, return 28 (31, 34, 37) sts from st holder to working needle. Keeping first and last 6 sts in garter st, work in St st until front measures 8 (9, 9¾, 10½)" from beg, ending with a WS row and remembering to work buttonholes as required at appropriate intervals.

Neck shaping: K8 (8, 9, 9) sts and place on holder to be used later for neck band. Work across rem sts. Cont in est patt and AT SAME TIME work ssk at neck edge every RS row until 15 (17, 19, 21) sts rem.

Work even until front measures same as back, ending with WS row. Join to right back shoulder using 3-needle BO (page 58).

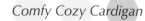

LEFT FRONT

With RS facing you, return 28 (31, 34, 37) sts from st holder to working needle. Keeping first and last 6 sts in garter st, work in St st until front measures 8 (9, 9¾, 10½)" from beg, ending with a WS row and remembering to work buttonholes as required at appropriate intervals.

Neck shaping: Patt across to last 8 (8, 9, 9) sts and place these sts on st holder to be used later for neck band. Cont in est patt and AT SAME TIME work K2tog at neck edge every RS row until 15 (17, 19, 21) sts rem.

Work even until front measures same as back, ending with WS row. Join to left back shoulder using 3-needle BO.

SLEEVES

CO 28 (30, 32, 34) sts.

Rows 1–8: Knit, marking first row as RS.

Beg working in St st and AT SAME TIME, work incs at each end on fifth row and every fourth row thereafter as follows: K1, M1, knit to last st, M1, K1. Work incs until you have 44 (50, 56, 60) sts.

Work even until sleeve measures 6 (6½, 7½, 8½)", ending with WS row. BO all sts. Work second sleeve in same manner.

NECK BAND

Row 1: With RS facing you, sl 8 (8, 9, 9) sts from right front holder to needle, attach yarn and PU 14 (15, 15, 16) sts along right neck edge, K20 (21, 22, 23) from back st holder, PU 14 (15, 15, 16) sts along left neck edge, K8 (8, 9, 9) sts from left front st holder—64 (67, 70, 73) sts.

Rows 2–4: Knit.

Row 5 (buttonhole row): K3, YO, knit to last 4 sts, YO, K2tog, K2.

Rows 6 and 7: Knit.

BO all sts on WS.

FINISHING

Sew buttons on appropriate side over buttonholes that won't be needed, closing up buttonholes as you do so. Sew in sleeves (see "Flat Seam Assembly" on page 59). Weave in all ends. Block if desired.

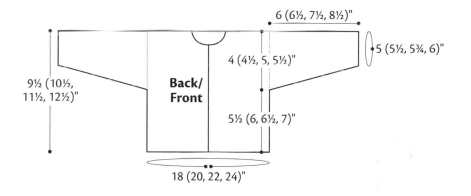

Grammy's Favorite Ensemble

This quick-to-knit baby set is absolutely perfect for little ones. The shaping and higher cuff on these booties give them an extra-special advantage—they actually stay put on Baby's feet! Since these mittens have no thumbs, babies can play with their fingers inside the mittens while keeping their hands warm. And no more struggling to put the mittens on—longer, larger cuffs fit perfectly over outerwear. A matching earflap hat adds the perfect final touch.

SKILL LEVEL
Easy ◼◼◻◻

SIZES
To fit: Up to 6 months

Booties: Approx 3¼" foot length

Thumbless mittens: Approx 2½" from top of mitten to wrist

Hat: Approx 15" circumference

MATERIALS
Yarn: 1 skein of Merino Super DK from Sandy's Palette (100% superwash merino wool; 100 g/ 3.5 oz; 246 yds/224 m) in color Nations Pride; *OR* approx 246 yds of equivalent DK-weight yarn

3

Needles: Size 4 (3.5 mm) straight, 16"-long circular, and double-pointed needles, or size to attain gauge

Notions: 1 stitch marker, 2 stitch holders

GAUGE
5½ sts and 8 rows = 1" in St st

BOOTIES
Beg at sole and using straight needles, CO 26 sts.

Rows 1, 3, 5, 7, and 9: Knit.

Row 2: K1, M1, K11, (M1, K1) twice, M1, K11, M1, K1—31 sts.

Row 4: K2, M1, K11, M1, K2, M1, K3, M1, K11, M1, K2—36 sts.

Row 6: K3, M1, K11, M1, K4, M1, K4, M1, K11, M1, K3—41 sts.

Row 8: K4, M1, K11, M1, K5, M1, K6, M1, K11, M1, K4—46 sts.

Row 10: K5, M1, K11, M1, K7, M1, K7, M1, K11, M1, K5—51 sts.

Rows 11, 13, 15, and 17: Knit.

Rows 12, 14, 16, and 18: Purl.

Instep

Row 1: K29, ssk, turn.

Rows 2, 4, 6, 8, 10, 12, and 14: Sl 1, P7, P2tog, turn.

Rows 3, 5, 7, 9, 11, and 13: Sl 1, K7, ssk, turn.

Row 15: Sl 1, K7, ssk, knit to end of row, turn.

Row 16: P21, P2tog, purl to end of row—35 sts.

Cuff

Work in garter st for 19 rows, ending with RS row.

BO all sts knitwise on WS.

Finishing

Sew center back and bottom sole seam (see "Flat Seam Assembly" on page 59). Weave in all ends.

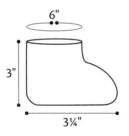

Top Shaping

Row 1: (RS) *K1, ssk, K12, K2tog, K1; rep from *—32 sts.

Row 2: *P1, P2tog, P10, P2tog tbl, P1; rep from *—28 sts.

Row 3: *K1, ssk, K8, K2tog, K1; rep from *—24 sts.

Row 4: *P1, P2tog, P6, P2tog tbl, P1; rep from *—20 sts.

Row 5: *K1, ssk, K4, K2tog, K1; rep from *—16 sts.

Row 6: *P1, P2tog, P2, P2tog tbl, P1; rep from *—12 sts.

Row 7: *K1, ssk, K2tog, K1; rep from *—8 sts.

Cut yarn, leaving approx 12" tail. Thread tail through rem 8 sts, pull tight, and secure. Sew side seam of mitten (see "Flat Seam Assembly"). Weave in all ends.

THUMBLESS MITTENS

Beg at cuff and using straight needles, CO 36 sts.

Rows 1–10: Knit, marking first row as RS.

Rows 11–22: Work in St st.

Row 23 (RS): *K2tog, rep from * across row—18 sts.

Rows 24–32: Knit.

Row 33 (RS): K1f&b in each st—36 sts.

Rows 34–50: Beg with purl row, work in St st.

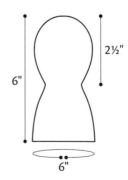

HAT

Earflaps (Make 2.)

Beg with ties and using straight or double-pointed needles, CO 3 sts. Work in garter st for 10".

Work earflaps as follows:

Row 1 (RS): K1, M1, knit to last st, M1, K1.

Row 2: Knit.

Rep last 2 rows until you have 17 sts, ending with WS row.

Work 24 rows even in garter st, ending with WS row.

Cut yarn and place sts on st holder.

Body of Hat

Beg at cuff and using 16"-long circular needle, CO and work sts from holders as follows: CO 11 sts for one half of back, K17 from holder for first earflap, CO 28 sts for front, K17 from holder for second earflap, CO 11 sts for other half of back—84 sts. Join, being careful not to twist sts, pm to denote beg of rnd.

Rnds 1, 3, 5, 7, 9, 11, 13, 15, 17, and 19: Purl.

Rnds 2, 4, 6, 8, 10, 12, 14, 16, and 18: Knit.

Rnds 20–27: Knit.

Rnds 28 and 30: Purl.

Rnd 29: Knit.

Rnds 31–37: Knit.

Rnd 38: Purl.

Rnd 39: Knit.

Rnd 40: Purl.

Crown

Work decs as follows, switching to dpns when necessary.

Rnd 1: *K5, K2tog, rep from * around—72 sts.

Rnd 2 and all even-numbered rnds: Knit.

Rnd 3: *K4, K2tog, rep from * around—60 sts.

Rnd 5: *K3, K2tog, rep from * around—48 sts.

Rnd 7: *K2, K2tog, rep from * around—36 sts.

Rnd 9: *K1, K2tog, rep from * around—24 sts.

Rnd 11: *K2tog, rep from * around—12 sts.

Rnd 13: *K2tog, rep from * around—6 sts.

Rnd 15: K1, K2tog twice, K1—4 sts.

Work I-cord for approx 3".

Cut yarn, thread through rem sts on needle, pull tight, and secure.

Finishing

Make an overhand knot with I-cord. Weave in all ends.

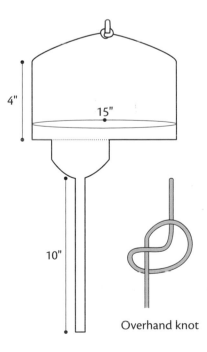

Overhand knot

Party-Time Jumper

What little girl wouldn't feel like a princess in this adorable party jumper? It makes special occasions even more special. I chose a hand-painted wool yarn, but this design would be equally charming in a solid color or in cotton yarn. The I-cord trim adds extra interest to both the yoke and the straps.

SKILL LEVEL

Intermediate ◼◼◼◻

SIZES

To fit: Up to 3 (6, 12, 18) months

Finished chest measurement: 18 (19, 20, 21)"

Length from underarm: 11 (12, 13, 14)"

MATERIALS

Yarn: 2 (3, 3, 4) skeins of Fingering Weight from Claudia Hand Painted Yarns (100% merino wool; 50 g/1.75 oz; 175 yds/160 m) in color Watermelon; *OR* approx 350 (420, 500, 580) yds of equivalent fingering-weight yarn ⑪

Needles: Size 2 (2.75 mm) straight and 24"-long circular needles, or size to attain gauge

Notions: 1 stitch marker, 3 decorative buttons— approx 1" diameter

GAUGE

7½ sts and 10 rows = 1" in St st

BODICE

Using straight needles, CO 17 (20, 23, 26) sts.

Every row: Knit to last 3 sts, sl 3 wyif. Mark first row as RS row.

Work in est patt until piece measures 18 (19, 20, 21)", ending with WS row.

BO all sts. Sew CO edge to BO edge.

Pick-Up Hint!

Because I-cord is a horizontal tube, when you pick up stitches along the edge, you're actually picking up the "bar" before the first stitch of I-cord on the row. Hold the bodice with the RS facing you and I-cord at the top. Slightly tip the I-cord down so you're looking at the back of the I-cord and the WS of the bodice. Picking up in this manner makes the I-cord pop out more.

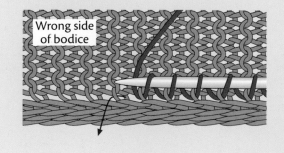

Wrong side of bodice

SKIRT

With WS of work facing you and with circular needle, PU 124 (132, 140, 148) sts under first row of purl loops just above one of the I-cord borders.

Turn work so RS is facing you. Pm to denote beg of rnd. Attach yarn and work skirt section as follows:

Next rnd: *K1, K1f&b in next st; rep from * around—186 (198, 210, 222) sts.

Work in St st (knit every rnd) until piece measures 10½ (11½, 12½, 13½)" from top band or ½" less than desired finished length.

Bottom Border

Rnds 1 and 3: Purl.

Rnds 2 and 4: Knit.

BO all sts purlwise.

STRAPS (MAKE 2)

Using straight needles, CO 12 (15, 15, 18) sts.

All rows: Knit to last 3 sts, wyif sl 3.

Work in est patt until strap measures 7 (8, 9, 10)".

BO all sts.

FINISHING

Sew straps to inside of front and back bodice along bottom of I-cord. Weave in all ends. Block if desired.

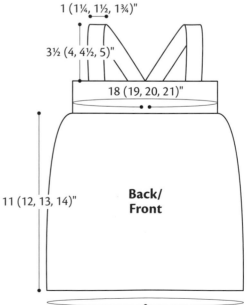

1 (1¼, 1½, 1¾)"

3½ (4, 4½, 5)"

18 (19, 20, 21)"

11 (12, 13, 14)"

Back/ Front

24¾ (26½, 28, 29½)"

Two Bibs

Who says a knitted bib can't be both practical and cute at the same time? These are! Knit in garter stitch using cotton yarn, the bibs are super absorbent as well as easy to care for—a perfect combination!

SKILL LEVEL
Easy ◖■□□

SIZE
Approx 7½" x 7½", excluding ties

MATERIALS

Yarn: Street from Lang Yarns (100% cotton; 50 g/ 1.75 oz; 115 yds/105 m) **3**

Pink bib 1 skein in color 59; *OR* approx 100 yds of DK weight

Blue bib 1 skein in color 10; *OR* approx 100 yds of DK weight

Needles: Size 6 (4 mm) circular needle (24" long), or size to attain gauge

Notions: 2 stitch markers

GAUGE
5½ sts and 10 rows = 1" in garter st

"PRETTY IN PINK" BIB

CO 50 sts, pm; CO 40 sts, pm, CO 50 sts—140 sts.

Row 1 (RS): Knit to 2 sts before marker, K2tog, sm, K2tog, knit to 2 sts before marker, K2tog, sm, K2tog, knit to end of row.

Row 2: Knit.

Work last 2 rows 2 more times, ending with WS row.

Neck Shaping

Row 1 (RS): K1, K2tog, knit to 2 sts before marker, K2tog, sm, K2tog, knit to 2 sts before marker, K2tog, sm, K2tog, knit to last 3 sts, K2tog, K1.

Row 2: Knit.

Work last 2 rows 8 more times, ending with WS row.

Center Section

Row 1 (RS): Knit to 2 sts before marker, K2tog, sm, K2tog, knit to 2 sts before marker, K2tog, sm, K2tog, knit to end of row.

Row 2: Knit.

Work last 2 rows until 2 sts rem between the 2 st markers, ending with WS row and removing markers on last row.

Next row: K20, K2tog and stop at this point. There should be 21 sts on right needle and 22 on left needle. Fold knitting so that RS are tog. Join sections using 3-needle BO (page 58) with this simple adjustment: On first set of sts worked, knit first st in front needle tog with first 2 sts on back needle.

Ties (Make 2.)

With RS facing you, PU 4 sts along top-left side of bib.

Next row (WS): K1, K2tog, K1—3 sts.

Work in garter st on 3 rem sts until tie measures 10", ending with WS row. BO all sts.

Rep on top-right edge.

Finishing

Weave in all ends.

"BLUE BOY" BIB

CO 20 sts.

Row 1 (RS): Knit.

Row 2: K1, M1, knit to last st, M1, K1.

Work last 2 rows until you have 40 sts, ending with WS row.

Work even in garter st as est until piece measures 7½" from CO row, ending with WS row.

Top Shaping

Row 1 (RS): K15, BO 10 sts; attach second yarn and K15.

Row 2: Knit.

Working each side at same time with separate yarns, cont as follows:

Row 1: K1, K2tog, knit to last 3 sts, K2tog, K1.

Row 2: Knit.

Work last 2 rows until 5 sts rem, ending with row 2.

Next row: K1, K3tog, K1—3 sts.

Ties (Make 2.)

Work in garter st as est on 3 rem sts until each tie measures 10". BO all sts.

Finishing

Weave in all ends.

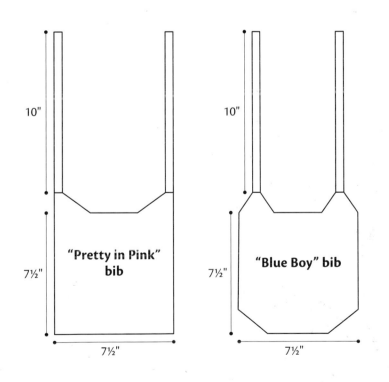

10"

10"

7½"   "Pretty in Pink" bib   7½"   "Blue Boy" bib

7½"   7½"

Cables and Lace Blanket

Why not welcome a new little one in your life with this beautiful blanket? It's sure to become a family heirloom that will be handed down from generation to generation.

SKILL LEVEL

Intermediate ◼◼◼◻

SIZE

Approx 33" x 38" when blocked

MATERIALS

Yarn: 8 skeins of Dream Baby DK from Plymouth Yarn Company Inc. (50% acrylic, 50% nylon; 50 g/1.75 oz; 183 yds/167 m) in color 100; *OR* approx 1400 yards of equivalent DK-weight yarn ③

Needles: Size 6 (4 mm) circular needle (29" or longer), or size to attain gauge

Notions: Cable needle

GAUGE

5½ sts and 9 rows = 1" in garter st

1 patt rep = approx 3¼" in width

CABLE AND LACE PATTERN

(Multiple of 20 sts plus 4 sts)

C6F: Sl 3 sts to cn and hold at front, K3, K3 from cn.

Row 1: *K4, P1, K3, P1, K6, P1, K3, P1, rep from * to last 4 sts, K4.

Row 2: K4, *K1, P3, K1, P6, K1, P3, K5, rep from * across row.

Row 3: *K4, P1, YO, sl 1-K2tog-psso, YO, P1, C6F, P1, YO, sl 1-K2tog-psso, YO, P1; rep from * to last 4 sts, K4.

Row 4: Rep row 2.

Row 5: Rep row 1.

Row 6: Rep row 2.

Row 7: *K4, P1, YO, sl 1-K2tog-psso, YO, P1, K6, P1, YO, sl 1-K2tog-psso, YO, P1; rep from * to last 4 sts, K4.

Row 8: Rep row 2.

Rep rows 1–8 for patt.

BLANKET

CO 204 sts.

Knit 6 rows, marking first row as RS row.

Work in cable and lace patt until 37" long or 1" short of desired finished length, ending with row 4 of patt.

Knit 5 rows. BO loosely on WS.

FINISHING

Weave in all ends. Block if desired.

Earflap Hat

Beginning with the I-cord ties on the earflaps, this hat is knit in one piece all the way up to the I-cord knot at the top! There are no seams to irritate Baby's head. Omit the optional flower and you have a hat that's equally fetching for a little boy.

SKILL LEVEL

Easy ◼◼☐☐

SIZE

Approx 16" circumference

MATERIALS

Yarn: 1 skein of Fingering 55 Silk from Claudia Hand Painted Yarns (55% silk, 45% merino wool; 50 g/1.75 oz, 175 yds/160 m) in color Shells on the Beach; *OR* approx 160 yds of equivalent fingering-weight yarn ⓵

Needles: Size 2 (2.75 mm) double-pointed and 16"-long circular needles, or size to attain gauge

Notions: 1 stitch marker, 2 stitch holders

GAUGE

7 sts and 10 rows = 1" in St st

TIES AND EARFLAPS (MAKE 2.)

Using dpns, CO 5 sts. Work 10" in I-cord (see "I-Cord" on page 59).

Work earflap as follows:

Row 1 (RS): K2, M1, K1, M1, K2—7 sts.

Rows 2–4: Knit.

Row 5: K2, M1, K3, M1, K2—9 sts.

Rows 6–8: Knit.

Row 9: K2, M1, K5, M1, K2—11 sts.

Rows 10–12: Knit.

Row 13: K2, M1, K7, M1, K2—13 sts.

Rows 14–16: Knit.

Row 17: K2, M1, K9, M1, K2—15 sts.

Rows 18–20: Knit.

Row 21: K2, M1, K11, M1, K2—17 sts.

Rows 22–24: Knit.

Row 25: K2, M1, K13, M1, K2—19 sts.

Rows 26–28: Knit.

Row 29: K2, M1, K15, M1, K2—21 sts.

Rows 30–40: Knit. Cut yarn and place sts on st holder.

Make second earflap in same fashion but leave sts on needle; do not cut yarn.

BODY OF HAT

Rnd 1: K21 from needle for first earflap to circular needle, CO 38 sts for front, K21 from holder for second earflap, CO 25 sts for back—105 sts. Pm to denote beg of rnd.

Rnds 2–12: Beg with purl row, work in garter st.

Work in St st until body of hat measures 5" from CO edge.

Crown

Work decs as follows, switching to dpns when necessary. See "Double Decrease (ddc)" on page 58.

Rnd 1: *K6, ddc, K6; rep from * around—91 sts.

Rnd 2 and all even-numbered rnds: Knit.

Rnd 3: *K5, ddc, K5; rep from * around—77 sts.

Rnd 5: *K4, ddc, K4; rep from * around—63 sts.

Rnd 7: *K3, ddc, K3; rep from * around—49 sts.

Rnd 9: *K2, ddc, K2; rep from * around—35 sts.

Rnd 11: *K1, ddc, K1; rep from * around—21 sts.

Rnd 13: Ddc around—7 sts.

Next row: K1, K2tog, K1, K2tog, K1—5 sts. Place all sts on 1 needle.

Work approx 2½" in I-cord over rem 5 sts. Cut yarn, leaving approx 4" tail. Thread through sts on needle, pull tight, and secure.

Make an overhand knot (see illustration on page 21) in I-cord. Weave in all ends.

FINISHING

Optional Flower

CO 12 sts.

Row 1: Knit.

Row 2: K1f&b in each st—24 sts.

Row 3: Knit.

Row 4: K1f&b in each st—48 sts.

Rows 5 and 6: Knit.

Row 7: K1, *YO, K1, rep from * across row.

BO all sts and cut yarn, leaving 6" tail.

Referring to photo above, twist piece around itself to form flower, and using tails from CO and BO, sew flower tog. Sew flower to hat.

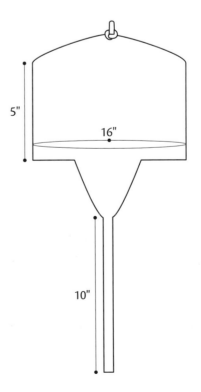

5"

16"

10"

Scalloped-Edge Jumper

Whatever the occasion, make it even more special for the small fry in your life with this adorable jumper. It's knit in one piece from the bottom up with what's traditionally considered sock yarn, proving yet again that there are many more things to make from sock yarn than socks!

SKILL LEVEL

Intermediate ◼◼◼◻

SIZES

To fit: Up to 6 (12, 18, 24) months

Finished chest measurement: 17 (19, 21, 23)"

Length from underarm: 12 (13, 14, 15)"

MATERIALS

Yarn: 1 (1, 2, 2) skeins of Berroco Sox Metallic from Berroco, Inc. (73% superwash wool, 25% nylon, 2% other fiber; 100 g/3.5 oz; 380 yds/347 m) in color 1361; *OR* approx 330 (375, 435, 500) yds of equivalent fingering-weight yarn (1)

Needles: Size 2 (2.75 mm) circular needles (16" and 24" long), or size to attain gauge

Notions: 1 stitch marker

GAUGE

7½ sts and 10 rows = 1" in St st

SKIRT

Using 24"-long circular needle, CO 152 (168, 184, 200) sts. Join, being careful not to twist sts, pm to denote beg of rnd.

Rnds 1, 3, and 5: Purl.

Rnds 2, 4, and 6: *K5 (6, 7, 8), ssk, K2tog, K5 (6, 7, 8), YO, K5, YO; rep from * around.

Beg body of skirt:

Rnd 1: *K14 (16, 18, 20), P5, rep from * around.

Rnd 2: *K5 (6, 7, 8), ssk, K2tog, K5 (6, 7, 8), YO, K5, YO; rep from * around.

Rep last 2 rnds until piece measures 4" from beg, ending with rnd 2.

Accurate Measuring

For easy, consistent, and accurate measuring, measure in the garter-stitch sections between the scallops.

First dec rnd: *K14 (16, 18, 20), P1, P2tog, P2; rep from * around—144 (160, 176, 192) sts.

Cont as follows:

Rnd 1: *K5 (6, 7, 8), ssk, K2tog, K5 (6, 7, 8), YO, K4, YO; rep from * around.

Rnd 2: *K14 (16, 18, 20), P4; rep from * around.

Rep last 2 rnds until piece measures 7" from beg, ending with rnd 1.

Second dec rnd: *K14 (16, 18, 20), P1, P2tog, P1; rep from * around—136 (152, 168, 184) sts.

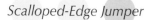

Cont as follows:

Rnd 1: *K5 (6, 7, 8), ssk, K2tog, K5 (6, 7, 8), YO, K3, YO; rep from * around.

Rnd 2: *K14 (16, 18, 20), P3; rep from * around.

Rep last 2 rnds until piece measures 10" from beg, ending with rnd 1.

Third dec rnd: *K14 (16, 18, 20), P1, P2tog; rep from * around—128 (144, 160, 176) sts.

Cont as follows:

Rnd 1: *K5 (6, 7, 8), ssk, K2tog, K5 (6, 7, 8) YO, K2, YO; rep from * around.

Rnd 2: *K14 (16, 18, 20), P2; rep from * around.

Rep last 2 rnds until piece measures 12 (13, 14, 15)" from beg, ending with rnd 1.

Fourth dec rnd: *K14 (16, 18, 20), P2tog; rep from * around—120 (136, 152, 168) sts.

Cut yarn. This completes body of jumper. Do not BO; leave sts on needle. Bodice is knitted onto body.

BODICE BORDER

Using knitted CO (page 56), CO 5 sts to left-hand needle.

Referring to "I-Cord" (page 59), work as follows: K4, ssk (using 1 st that you just CO and 1 st from sts at top of jumper), sl 5 sts just worked from right needle back to left needle. Rep this process until all sts from skirt top have been worked into border. BO 5 sts.

Sew BO and CO edges tog.

BODICE

With RS facing you, PU 120 (136, 152, 168) sts around back inside edge of I-cord border. See "Pick-Up Hint!" (page 22).

Work bodice as follows:

Rnds 1, 3, 5, 7, and 9: Purl.

Rnds 2, 4, 6, and 8: Knit.

BO sts using same method as for bodice border to make attached I-cord.

STRAPS (MAKE 2.)

CO 12 sts.

All rows: K9, sl 3 wyif.

Work est patt until strap measures 10 (11, 12, 13)" from beg.

BO all sts.

FINISHING

Sew straps to inside of front and back bodice along bottom of I-cord. Weave in all ends. Block if desired.

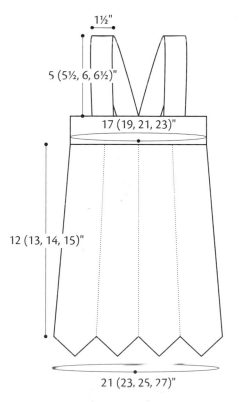

1½"

5 (5½, 6, 6½)"

17 (19, 21, 23)"

12 (13, 14, 15)"

21 (23, 25, 27)"

Tricolor Ensemble

If you're looking for an ensemble that isn't frilly and lacy, yet still has style to it, this is the one for you. I made it in vibrant colors, perfect for a little boy. Who says baby items have to be pastel?

SKILL LEVEL

Easy ◼◼◻◻

SIZES

To fit: Up to 6 months

Booties: Approx 3¼" foot length

Thumbless mittens: Approx 2½" from top of mitten to wrist

Hat: 13 (14, 15)" circumference

Sweater: Up to 6 (12, 18) months

Finished chest measurement: 18 (20, 22)"

Back length: 11 (11½, 12)"

Sleeve length: 6½ (7, 7½)"

MATERIALS

Yarn: Comfort DK from Berroco, Inc. (50% nylon, 50% acrylic; 50 g/1.75 oz; 178 yds/165 m); *OR* equivalent DK-weight yarn 🧶 **3**

A 2 (2, 3) skeins in color 2753 (blue); *OR* approx 320 (345, 380) yds

B 2 skeins in color 2727 (brown); *OR* approx 210 (230, 260) yds

C 2 skeins in color 2740 (green); *OR* approx 190 (220, 250) yds

Needles: Size 4 (3.5 mm) straight, double-pointed, and circular needles (16" long for hat and 24" long for sweater)

Notions: 2 stitch markers, 3 stitch holders, yarn bobbins (optional), 1 button for sweater—½" diameter

GAUGE

6 sts and 9 rows = 1" in St st

THUMBLESS MITTENS

Beg at cuff, using straight needles and B, CO 36 sts.

Rows 1 and 3 (RS): With B, purl.

Rows 2 and 4: With B, knit.

Rows 5 and 7: With C, knit.

Rows 6 and 8: With C, purl.

Rows 9, 10, and 12: With B, knit.

Row 11: With B, purl.

Rows 13 and 15: With C, knit.

Rows 14 and 16: With C, purl. Cut C.

Row 17: With B, *K2tog, rep from * across row—18 sts.

Rows 18–23: With B, knit.

Row 24: K1f&b in each st—36 sts. Cut B.

Rows 25–40: Change to A, beg with a knit row, work in St st.

Top Shaping

Row 1: (RS) *K1, ssk, K12, K2tog, K1; rep from *—32 sts.

Row 2: *P1, P2tog, P10, P2tog tbl, P1; rep from *—28 sts.

Row 3: *K1, ssk, K8, K2tog, K1; rep from *—24 sts.

Row 4: *P1, P2tog, P6, P2tog tbl, P1, rep from *—20 sts.

Row 5: *K1, ssk, K4, K2tog, K1; rep from *—16 sts.

Row 6: *P1, P2tog, P2, P2tog tbl, P1; rep from *—12 sts.

Row 7: *K1, ssk, K2tog, K1; rep from *—8 sts.

Cut yarn, leaving approx 12" tail. Thread tail through rem 8 sts, pull tight, and secure. Sew side seam of mitten (see "Flat Seam Assembly" on page 59). Weave in all ends.

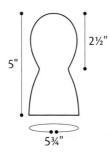

BOOTIES

Starting at sole of bootie, using straight needles and A, CO 26 sts.

Rows 1, 3, 5, 7, and 9 (RS): Knit.

Row 2: K1, M1, K11, (M1, K1) twice, M1, K11, M1, K1—31 sts.

Row 4: K2, M1, K11, M1, K2, M1, K3, M1, K11, M1, K2—36 sts.

Row 6: K3, M1, K11, M1, K4, M1, K4, M1, K11, M1, K3—41 sts.

Row 8: K4, M1, K11, M1, K5, M1, K6, M1, K11, M1, K4—46 sts.

Row 10: K5, M1, K11, M1, K7, M1, K7, M1, K11, M1, K5—51 sts.

Rows 11, 13, 15, and 17: Knit.

Rows 12, 14, 16, and 18: Purl.

Instep

Row 1: K29, ssk, turn.

Rows 2, 4, 6, 8, 10, 12, and 14: Sl 1, P7, P2tog, turn work.

Rows 3, 5, 7, 9, 11, and 13: Sl 1, K7, ssk, turn work.

Row 15: Sl 1, K7, ssk, knit to end of row.

Row 16: P21, P2tog, purl to end of row—35 sts. Cut A.

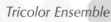

Cuff

Rows 1, 2, and 4: With B, knit.

Row 3: With B, purl.

Rows 5 and 7: With C, knit.

Rows 6 and 8: With C, purl.

Rows 9–16: Rep rows 1–8.

Rows 17–19: Rep rows 1–3.

BO all sts on WS. Cut tail, leaving about 18" for seaming.

Finishing

Sew center back and bottom sole seam (see "Flat Seam Assembly" on page 59). Weave in all ends.

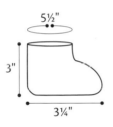

5½"

3"

3¼"

EARFLAP HAT

Ties and Flaps (Make 2.)

Using straight needles and C, CO 4 sts. Work 10" in I-cord (page 59) for ties. Turn work, knit back on these 4 sts.

Work earflaps as follows:

Row 1: (RS) K1, M1, knit to last st, M1, K1.

Row 2: Knit.

Rep rows 1 and 2 until there are 20 (22, 22) sts, ending with WS row.

Knit 8 (10, 10) rows even. Cut yarn and place sts on holder.

Rep for second earflap.

Bottom of Hat

Using 16"-long circular needle and B, CO and work sts from holders as follows: CO 7 (8, 10) sts for one half of back, with RS of flap facing you, K20 (22, 22) from holder for first earflap, CO 23 (24, 27) for front, with RS of flap facing you, K20 (22, 22) from holder for second earflap, CO 7 (8, 10) sts for second half of back—77 (84, 91) sts. Join, being careful not to twist sts, pm to denote beg of rnd.

Rnds 1–4: With B, purl.

Rnds 5–8: With C, knit.

Rnd 9: With B, knit.

Rnds 10–13: With B, purl.

Rnds 14–17: With C, knit. Cut C.

Rnd 18: With B, knit.

Rnds 19–21: With B, purl. Cut B.

Body of Hat

Attach A and work in St st until hat measures 5 (5, 5½)" from CO edge.

Accurate Measuring

In order to get an accurate measurement, stretch the piece out slightly.

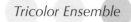

Crown

Work decs as follows, switching to dpns when necessary.

Rnd 1: K4 (4, 5), ddc, *K8 (9, 10), ddc; rep from * around to last 4 (5, 5) sts, K4 (5, 5).

Rnd 2 and all even-numbered rnds: Knit.

Rnd 3: K3 (3, 4), ddc, *K6 (7, 8), ddc; rep from * to last 3 (4, 4) sts, K3 (4, 4).

Cont dec as est, knitting 2 less sts between decs until 7 sts rem. Cut yarn, leaving approx 6" tail. Thread yarn through rem sts, pull tight, and secure.

Finishing

Weave in all ends. Block if desired.

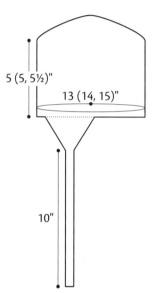

5 (5, 5½)"

13 (14, 15)"

10"

SWEATER

Using 24"-long circular needle and A, CO 114 (126, 138) sts.

Knit 10 rows, marking first row as RS.

Body

Keeping first and last 5 sts in garter st with A, beg working in stripe patt as follows:

Rows 1 and 3: With C, knit.

Rows 2 and 4: With C, purl.

Rows 5, 6, and 8: With B, knit.

Row 7: With B, purl.

Rep these 8 rows until piece measures 6 (6½, 7)" from beg, ending with either row 4 or row 8.

Divide for Front and Back

On next row, patt across 30 (33, 36) sts and place on st holder to be used later for right front, K54 (60, 66) sts for back, place rem 30 (33, 36) sts on second holder to be used later for left front. You will now be working back and forth.

Back

Cont in est stripe patt until back measures 11 (11½, 12)" from beg, ending with row 2 or row 6. Divide sts equally onto 3 st holders, with 18 (20, 22) sts on each holder.

Right Front

Return front sts back to working needle. Attach yarn and cont in est patt until front measures 9 (9¾, 10½)" from beg, ending with row 2 or row 6.

Neck shaping: Work 8 (9, 9) sts and place on holder to be used later for neck band. Work across rem sts. Cont in est patt and AT SAME TIME work ssk (or P2tog tbl as patt row dictates) at neck edge every RS row until 18 (20, 22) sts rem.

Work even until front measures same as back, ending with WS row. Join to right-back shoulder using 3-needle BO (page 58).

Left Front

With RS facing you, return the 30 (33, 36) sts from st holder to working needle. Cont in est patt until front measures 9 (9¾, 10½)" from beg, ending with row 1 or row 7.

Neck shaping: Patt across to last 8 (9, 9) sts and place these sts on st holder to be used later for neck band. Cont in est patt and AT SAME TIME work K2tog (or P2tog as patt row dictates) at neck edge every RS row until 18 (20, 22) sts rem.

Work even until front measures same as back, ending with WS row. Join to left-back shoulder using 3-needle BO.

Sleeves

Using dpns and A, PU 54 (60, 66) around armhole.

Knit 4 rnds.

Cont in St st and AT SAME TIME, work decs at both ends of next and every following fourth rnd as follows: K1, ssk, knit to last 3 sts, K2tog, K1. Work until 36 (40, 40) sts rem.

Work even until sleeve measures 5½ (6, 6½)" or 1" less than desired finished length. Work second sleeve in same manner.

Border

Rnds 1, 3, 5, and 7: Purl.

Rnds 2, 4, 6, and 8: Knit.

BO all sts purlwise.

Neck Band

Sl 5 border sts back on working needle. With RS facing you and A, knit the rem 3 (4, 4) sts from holder, PU 15 (17, 19) sts along right neck edge, K18 (20, 22) sts from back st holder, PU 15 (17, 19) sts from left-front st holder, K8 (9, 9) sts from rem st holder—64 (72, 78) sts.

Row 1 (buttonhole row on WS): K3, YO, K2tog, knit to last 5 sts, K2tog, YO, K3.

Rows 2–4: Knit.

BO all sts knitwise on WS.

Finishing

Sew button on appropriate side for boy or girl (right for girls, left for boys), closing up buttonhole on that side. Weave in all ends. Block if desired.

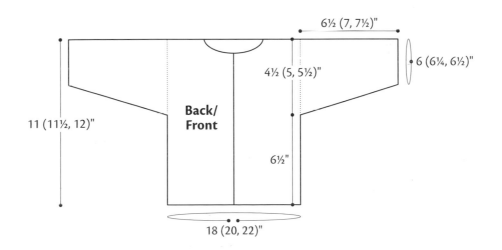

6½ (7, 7½)"

6 (6¼, 6½)"

4½ (5, 5½)"

11 (11½, 12)"

Back/ Front

6½"

18 (20, 22)"

Tricolor Blanket

Whether made as part of the tricolor ensemble or as a gift in itself, this blanket will be a welcome addition for any baby. Why not make it to match the colors in the child's room?

SKILL LEVEL

Easy ◗■□▭

SIZE

Approx 32" x 38" when blocked

MATERIALS

Yarn: Comfort DK from Berroco, Inc. (50% nylon, 50% acrylic; 50 g/1.75 oz; 178 yds/165 m) *OR* equivalent DK-weight yarn **[3]**

A 4 skeins in color 2753 (blue); *OR* approx 700 yds

B 3 skeins in color 2727 (brown); *OR* approx 500 yds

C 3 skeins in color 2740 (green); *OR* approx 470 yds

Needles: Size 5 (3.75 mm) circular needle (29" or longer), or size to attain gauge

Notions: 7 yarn bobbins

GAUGE

5½ sts and 8 rows = 1" in St st

BOTTOM BORDER

Using A, CO 170 sts.

Knit 14 rows.

Keeping first and last 12 sts in garter st in A, beg body of blanket as follows:

Rows 1 and 3 (RS): With C, knit.

Rows 2 and 4: With C, purl.

Rows 5 and 6: With B, knit.

Row 7: With B, purl.

Row 8: With B, knit.

These 8 rows form the stripe patt. Work rows 1–8 six more times; then rep rows 1–4 once more, ending with WS row.

Carrying Yarns Up the Side

Since you are only going up a short distance each time with the color changes, you can opt not to cut the yarn each time, which means you'll have fewer ends to weave in (a good thing, especially in a baby blanket). Simply make sure that you're twisting the yarns and carrying them up along the wrong side of the work on each row.

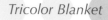

BLANKET CENTER

Maintaining the 12-st garter border on each side as well as keeping 38 sts on each side in est stripe patt, beg working center 70 sts in garter st with A.

Cont in this fashion until 23 more stripe sequences have been completed, ending with row 8.

Adding More Bobbins

You can continue carrying the yarns up from the individual stripe sequences as before by simply using a couple more bobbins. This does require a little more patience—you need to make sure that the yarns are wrapped to prevent holes—but the end result is well worth it.

TOP BORDER

Cutting yarns for center A section as well as left-hand side striped section (as it is lying), cont working striped patt sequence across entire blanket again, remembering to maintain 12-st garter border in A. Work an additional 7 stripe reps, ending with row 8. Then work rows 1–4 once more, ending with WS row.

Cut all yarns except strand of A that is now at start of row. Work 13 rows in garter st. BO all sts knitwise on WS.

FINISHING

Weave in all ends. Block if desired.

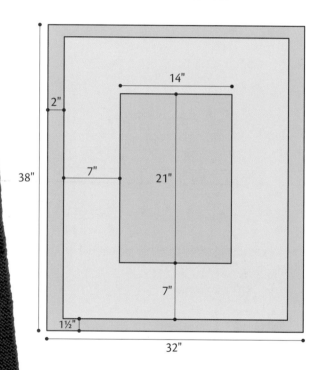

Comfy Hoodie

With the comfort and ease of a hooded sweatshirt, this hoodie is knit in the round and requires only minimal finishing. The garter-stitch bottom border allows for an easy, loose fit. It's so quick to knit, you'll want to make several! I chose to use one of the many self-striping yarns that are so popular.

SKILL LEVEL

Intermediate ◖■■◻

SIZES

To fit: Up to 6 (12, 18, 24) months

Finished chest measurement: 18 (20, 22, 24)"

Back length: 10 (11, 12, 13)"

Sleeve length: 6 (6½, 7½, 8½)" from underarm

MATERIALS

Yarn: 1 (1, 2, 2) skeins of Step 6-Ply from Austermann Yarns (75% superwash wool, 25% nylon; 150 g/5.25 oz; 401 yds/364 m) in color 603; OR approx 380 (400, 425, 455) yds of equivalent DK-weight yarn (3)

Needles: Size 4 (3.5 mm) straight, double-pointed, and 24"-long circular needles, or size to attain gauge

Notions: 4 stitch markers (1 a different color for beg of rnd), 2 stitch holders, size F/5 (3.75 mm) crochet hook, 1 button—½" in diameter

GAUGE

6 sts and 9 rows = 1" in St st

BODY

Beg at bottom and using 24"-long circular needle, CO 54 (60, 66, 72) sts, pm, CO 54 (60, 66, 72) sts—108 (120, 132, 144) sts. Join, being careful not to twist sts, and pm to denote beg of rnd.

Work 8 (8, 10, 10) rnds of garter st.

Change to St st and work until piece measures 5 (5, 6, 6)" from beg. Drop working yarn but leave attached for later use.

POCKET

Lay sweater with front side facing up. Count in toward front of sweater 8 (8, 10, 10) sts from each marker. Follow that st down and place marker in center of it, 1 row above last garter-st ridge. Insert crochet hook through marked st from INSIDE to OUTSIDE of sweater on left side as it lies. Using separate yarn, pull approx 18" tail of yarn to inside of work. Leaving yarn inside sweater, insert hook from outside to inside in first st to left of marked st on RS of sweater front as it lies and pull up yarn, leaving approx 4" tail of yarn on inside of sweater. Working in same row and moving to left, insert crochet hook in each st across and pick up loop/st. When you get more than can fit on crochet hook, transfer them to size 4 straight needle. *When you transfer sts from hook to needle, be careful not to twist sts.* You should have total of 38 (44, 46, 52) sts when you reach opposite side (stopping where you originally inserted yarn).

Next row (WS): K5, pm, purl to last 5 sts, pm, K5.

Beg pocket:

Rows 1 and 3 (RS): Knit.

Rows 2 and 4: K5, purl to last 5 sts, K5.

Row 5: K5, ssk, knit to last 7 sts, K2tog, K5.

Row 6: K5, purl to last 5 sts, K5.

Row 7: Knit.

Row 8: K5, purl to last 5 sts, K5.

Rep rows 5–8 until 26 (32, 34, 40) sts rem, ending with row 8.

Work 8 (8, 12, 12) rows even. Cut yarn. Leave these sts on straight needle.

Return to circular needle and work body of sweater until it's same length as pocket, ending at end of a rnd.

JOINING POCKET TO BODY

K14 (14, 16, 16), bring pocket needle parallel with circular needle, knit first st of pocket tog with next st of body, knit second st from pocket with next st of body, rep in this fashion until all pocket sts have been knit tog with corresponding st of body, knit around to end of rnd.

Work even on body until it measures 6 (6½, 7½, 8)" from beg.

Next rnd: Knit to 6 sts beyond halfway marker, place 6 sts from each side of this marker on st holder (12 sts total), knit to 6 sts beyond beg-of-rnd marker, place 6 sts from each side of this marker (12 sts total) on second st holder. Do not cut yarn.

SLEEVES

Using dpns, CO 36 (40, 42, 44) sts. Join, being careful not to twist sts, pm to denote beg of rnd. Work in garter st for 8 (8, 10, 10) rnds.

Inc rnd: K0 (2, 0, 1), *K3, M1, rep from * to last 0 (2, 1, 1) sts, K0 (2, 0, 1)—48 (52, 56, 60) sts.

Work in St st until sleeve measures 6 (6½, 7½, 8½)" from beg, ending last rnd by working 6 sts beyond beg-of-rnd marker. Cut yarn, leaving approx 18" tail. Place 6 sts from either side of marker on st holder (12 sts total). Work second sleeve in same manner.

JOINING SLEEVES TO BODY

Knit across front of sweater, pm, knit first sleeve onto body needle, pm, knit across back of sweater, pm, knit second sleeve onto body, pm (making it different color than other markers to denote beg of rnd)—156 (176, 196, 216) sts.

Work 2 (2, 3, 3) rnds even.

Raglan Shaping

Rnd 1 (dec rnd): *K1, ssk, knit to 3 sts before marker, K2tog, K1; rep from * around—148 (168, 188, 208) sts.

Rnd 2: Knit.

Work last 2 rnds 3 (3, 4, 4) more times—124 (144, 156, 176) sts at end of last rep.

Pm on each side of center 10 (10, 10, 10) sts on front.

Cont to dec as est and AT SAME TIME work center-front sts in garter st. (If you purl them on rnd 1, then you'll have all your thinking done on one row and have a "no-brainer" row…easier to keep track of things!) Work dec as est for 9 more rnds, ending with rnd 1—84 (104, 116, 136) sts.

PLACKET DIVISION

Knit to marked placket sts, then knit placket sts. Turn work. This is your new beg of row. You'll now be working back and forth. K10 (10, 10, 10), purl to end of row. CO 10 (10, 10, 10) sts at end of row—94 (114, 126, 146) sts.

Keeping first and last 10 (10, 10, 10) sts in garter st, work rem sts in St st and cont decs as est on RS rows until you have 78 (82, 86, 90) sts, ending with WS row.

Buttonhole row 1: Work dec as est to last 10 sts, K4, BO 2 sts, K3.

Buttonhole row 2: K4, CO 2 sts, K4, purl to end of row.

Work 2 more rows in est patt dec—62 (66, 70, 74) sts.

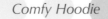

NECK BAND

BO 5 sts (for all sizes) at beg of next 2 rows, knit to end.

Work in garter st for 6 (6, 8, 8) more rows, removing markers—52 (56, 60, 64) sts.

HOOD

Inc row: K10, pm, *K2, M1; rep from * to last 10 sts, pm, K10—68 (74, 80, 86) sts.

Keeping first and last 10 sts in garter st and rem of sts in St st, work even until hood measures 8 (8, 9, 10)", ending with WS row.

Next row: K34 (37, 40, 43) sts, stopping in middle of row. Cut yarn, leaving approx 24" tail.

FINISHING

Fold hood sts with WS tog and graft top of hood tog with Kitchener st (page 60).

Use Kitchener st to sew underarm sts tog. Note that you may have a small hole on each side of underarm sts. This is common; just weave around hole with yarn, pull tog, and secure on inside.

Sew CO of placket to WS of corresponding sts on other placket side. Weave in all ends. Sew on button.

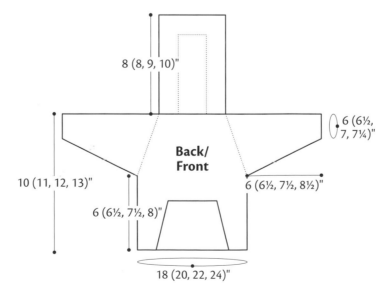

8 (8, 9, 10)"

6 (6½, 7, 7¼)"

10 (11, 12, 13)"

Back/ Front

6 (6½, 7½, 8½)"

6 (6½, 7½, 8)"

18 (20, 22, 24)"

Quick-Knit Vest

Too warm for a sweater, yet Baby needs a little something to keep out the chill? Why not a vest? Basic in styling, this vest lets the wonderful yarn do the design work. It's knit in one piece—the only finishing is at the shoulders and sewing on the buttons!

SKILL LEVEL

Easy ◼◼◻◻

SIZES

To fit: Up to 6 (12, 18, 24) months

Finished chest measurement: 18 (20, 22, 24)"

Back length: 9½ (10½, 11½, 12½)"

MATERIALS

Yarn: 2 (2, 3, 4) skeins of Rhythm Superwash from JojoLand Yarns (100% superwash wool; 50 g/1.76 oz; 100 yds/100 m) in color 71; OR approx 180 (220, 260, 300) yds of equivalent DK-weight yarn

Needles: Size 5 (3.75 mm) needles, or size to attain gauge, or size to attain gauge

Notions: 6 stitch markers, 2 stitch holders, 5 buttons—½" in diameter

GAUGE

5½ sts and 8 rows = 1" in St st

Design Notes

This vest is knit in one piece with the buttonhole/button bands knit at the same time. Therefore, it's important to remember to work the buttonhole rows at appropriate intervals. Buttonhole rows have been written for buttonholes worked on both bands. That way you can make this vest without knowing the baby's sex, and apply the buttons after he/she is born! Should you know the sex, simply work the buttonholes on the appropriate side (right for girls, left for boys) and omit them on the other side.

BORDER

Beg at lower edge, CO 106 (117, 128, 139) sts.

Rows 1 (RS)–4: Knit.

Row 5 (buttonhole row): K3, YO, K2tog, knit to last 4 sts, YO, K2tog, K2.

Rows 6–9: Knit.

Row 10 (WS): K6, pm, P16 (19, 22, 25), pm, K12, pm, P38 (43, 48, 53), pm, K12, pm, P16 (19, 22, 25), pm, K6.

BODY

Row 1 (RS): Knit.

Row 2: K6, sm, P16 (19, 22, 25), sm, K12, sm, P38 (43, 48, 53), sm, K12, sm, P16 (19, 22, 25), sm, K6.

Rep last 2 rows until piece measures 5½ (6, 6½, 7)" from beg, ending with WS row, and AT SAME TIME work buttonhole row every 16 (18, 20, 22) rows. There will be 8 (9, 10, 11) ridges between buttonholes. (Note: When counting rows/ridges between buttonholes, do not count the 2 rows/ 1 ridge where buttonhole was worked.)

DIVIDE FOR FRONT AND BACK

On next row, K25 (28, 31, 34) and place sts on st holder to be used later for right front, BO 6 sts for underarm section, K44 (49, 54, 59) sts for back, place rem 31 (34, 37, 40) sts on second holder to be used later for left-front and underarm section.

BACK

Beg with WS row, cont in St st while keeping garter-st borders as est until back measures 9½ (10½, 11½, 12½)" from beg, ending with WS row.

Divide sts onto 3 holders:

Holders 1 and 3: 12 (14, 16, 18) sts

Holder 2: 20 (21, 22, 23) sts

RIGHT FRONT

With WS facing you, return 25 (28, 31, 34) sts from st holder to working needle. Keeping garter-st borders as est, work in St st until front measures 7½ (8½, 9½, 10½)" from beg, ending with a WS row and remembering to work buttonholes as required at appropriate intervals.

Neck shaping: K8 (8, 9, 9) sts and place sts on st holder to be used later for neck band. Work across rem sts. Cont in est patt and AT SAME TIME work ssk at neck edge every RS row until 12 (14, 16, 18) sts rem.

Work even until front measures same as back, ending with WS row. Join to right-back shoulder using 3-needle BO (page 58).

LEFT FRONT

With RS facing you, return 31 (34, 37, 40) sts from st holder to working needle. Attach working yarn. BO 6 sts and knit to end of row.

Keeping garter-st borders as est, work in St st until front measures 7½ (8½, 9½, 10½)" from beg, ending with a WS row and remembering to work buttonholes as required at appropriate intervals.

Neck shaping: Patt across to last 8 (8, 9, 9) sts and place these sts on st holder to be used later for neck band. Cont in est patt and AT SAME TIME work K2tog at neck edge every RS row until 12 (14, 16, 18) sts rem.

Work even until front measures same as back, ending with WS row. Join to left-back shoulder using 3-needle BO.

NECK BAND

Row 1: With RS facing you, sl 8 (8, 9, 9) sts from right-front holder to needle. Attach yarn, PU 14 (15, 15, 16) sts along right neck edge, K20 (21, 22, 23) from back st holder, PU 14 (15, 15, 16) sts along left neck edge, K8 (8, 9, 9) sts from left-front st holder—64 (67, 70, 73) sts.

Rows 2–4: Knit.

Row 5 (buttonhole row): K3, YO, knit to last 4 sts, YO, K2tog, K2.

Rows 6 and 7: Knit.

BO all sts on WS.

FINISHING

Sew buttons on appropriate side over buttonholes that won't be needed, closing up buttonholes as you do so. Weave in all ends. Block if desired.

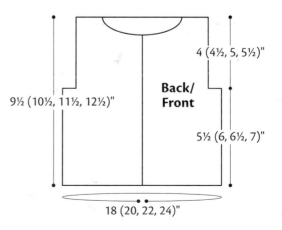

4 (4½, 5, 5½)"

Back/ Front

9½ (10½, 11½, 12½)"

5½ (6, 6½, 7)"

18 (20, 22, 24)"

Shoulder-Button Pullover

Who says a little one's sweater can't be fun? The six buttons on the shoulders not only add style, but make getting this pullover on and off a breeze! Knit in one piece up to the armholes, this great sweater is finished in no time at all.

SKILL LEVEL

Easy ◖■□▭

SIZES

To fit: Up to 6 (12, 18, 24) months

Finished chest measurement: 18 (20, 22, 24)"

Back length: 10½ (11¼, 12¼, 12¾)"

Sleeve length: 6 (6½, 7½, 8½)" from underarm

MATERIALS

Yarn: 1 (1, 2, 2) skeins of Mer-Made DK Weight from Blackberry Ridge Woolen Mill, Inc. (100% superwash wool; 128 g/4.5 oz; 275 yds/250 m) in color Tropical Fish; *OR* approx 250 (275, 310, 350) yds of equivalent DK-weight yarn [3]

Needles: Size 6 (4 mm) double-pointed and circular needles (24" long)

Notions: 1 stitch marker, 2 stitch holders, 6 buttons—½" in diameter

GAUGE

5½ sts and 7 rows = 1" in patt st

BOTTOM BORDER

Beg at bottom of sweater using circular needle, CO 100 (110, 120, 130) sts. Join, being careful not to twist sts, pm to denote beg of rnd.

Work 4 (4, 6, 6) rnds in garter st.

BODY

Rnd 1: Knit.

Rnd 2: K2, P1, *K4, P1; rep from * to last 2 sts, K2.

Rep last 2 rnds until piece measures 6 (6½, 7, 7½)" from beg, ending with rnd 1.

DIVIDE FOR FRONT AND BACK

On next row, patt across 50 (55, 60, 65) sts, place rem 50 (55, 60, 65) sts on st holder to be used later for front section.

Next row: Turn work and purl back. You will now work back and forth.

BACK

Row 1 (RS): K2, P1, *K4, P1; rep from * to last 2 sts, K2.

Row 2: Purl.

Rep last 2 rows until piece measures 3½ (4, 4½, 4½)" from dividing row, ending with WS row.

Button Bands

Next row: K14 (16, 18, 20) sts, place next 22 (23, 24, 25) sts on st holder, attach second skein of yarn and K14 (16, 18, 20) sts.

Working both sides AT SAME TIME, knit 4 rows.

BO on WS in knit.

Back Neck Band

With RS facing you, PU 3 sts along right shoulder band, K22 (23, 24, 25) from holder, PU 3 sts from left shoulder band—28 (29, 30, 31) sts.

Knit 4 rows.

BO all sts on WS.

FRONT

Return 50 (55, 60, 65) sts from holder to working needle. With RS facing you, attach yarn and work in est patt until front measures 2 (2½, 3, 3)" from dividing row, ending with WS row.

Neck Shaping

Work in est patt across 19 (21, 23, 25) sts, place next 12 (13, 14, 15) sts on holder, attach second skein and work in est patt across rem 19 (21, 23, 25) sts. Work *both* sides with separate yarns in est patt and AT SAME TIME dec 1 st at neck edge (ssk on right front and K2tog on left front) on every RS row until 14 (16, 18, 20) sts rem.

Work even until front measures same length as back to button bands, ending with RS row.

Buttonhole Bands

Work each side as follows:

Row 1 (WS): Knit.

Row 2: K2, YO, K2tog, K2 (3, 4, 5), YO, K2tog, K2 (3, 4, 5), YO, K2tog, K2.

Rows 3 and 4: Knit.

BO on WS in knit.

Neck Band

With RS facing you, PU 11 (12, 13, 14) sts along left-front neck edge (including 3 from buttonhole band), K12 (13, 14, 15) sts from front st holder, PU 11 (12, 13, 14) sts along right-front neck edge—34 (37, 40, 43) sts.

Knit 4 rows.

BO all sts kw on WS.

Overlap buttonhole bands over button bands and pin into place.

SLEEVES

Using dpns, with RS facing you and beg at underarm, PU 45 (50, 55, 55) sts around armhole edge, making sure to go through *both* layers of buttonhole bands. Pm to denote beg of rnd.

Rnd 1: K2, P1, *K4, P1, rep from * to last 2 sts, K2.

Rnd 2: Knit.

Rep last 2 rnds and AT SAME TIME while maintaining patt, dec 1 st at beg and end of every 4th rnd until 27 (30, 33, 33) sts rem, working decs as follows: K1, ssk, knit to last 3 sts, K2tog, K1.

Work even until sleeve measures 5½ (6, 7, 8)" or ½" less than desired sleeve length, ending with rnd 2.

Work cuff as follows:

Rnds 1 and 3: Purl.

Rnds 2 and 4: Knit.

BO all sts pw.

Rep to make second sleeve.

FINISHING

Sew buttons on to match buttonhole placement on shoulders. Weave in all ends.

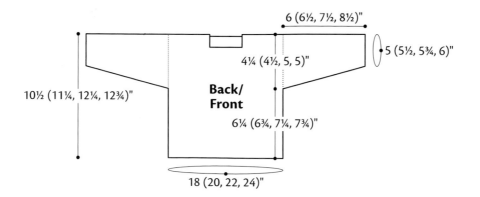

Abbreviations and Glossary

approx	approximately
beg	begin(ning)
BO	bind off
CC	contrasting color
ch	chain
cn	cable needle
CO	cast on
cont	continue(ing)(s)
ddc	double decrease—2 stitches decreased (page 58)
dec(s)	decrease(d)(ing)(s)
dpn(s)	double-pointed needle(s)
EOR	every other right-side row
est	established
g	grams
garter st	garter stitch (see page 56)
inc(s)	increase(d)(ing)(s)
K	knit
K1f&b	knit into front and back of same stitch—1 stitch increased (page 57)
K2tog	knit 2 stitches together—1 stitch decreased (page 57)
kw	knitwise
M1	make 1 stitch—1 stitch increased (page 57)
MC	main color
m	meters
mm	millimeters
oz	ounces
P	purl

P2tog	purl 2 stitches together as 1—1 stitch decreased
patt	pattern(s)
pm	place marker
psso	pass slipped stitch over
PU	pick up and knit
pw	purlwise
rem	remain(ing)
rep(s)	repeat(s)
rnd(s)	round(s)
RS	right side
sc	single crochet
sl	slip as if to purl unless otherwise instructed
sl 1-K2tog-psso	slip 1 stitch as if to knit, knit 2 stitches together, pass the slipped stitch over the 2 stitches knit together—2 stitches decreased
sm	slip marker
ssk	slip, slip, knit—1 stitch decreased (page 58)
st(s)	stitch(es)
St st	stockinette stitch (page 56)
tbl	through the back loop(s)
tog	together
WS	wrong side
wyib	with yarn in back
wyif	with yarn in front
yd(s)	yard(s)
YO	yarn over

Knitting Basics

Refer to the following guidelines for the basic techniques used for the projects in this book.

BASIC PATTERN STITCHES

Most of the designs in this book use these basic pattern stitches.

Garter Stitch

In the round: Knit one round, purl one round.

Back and forth: Knit every row.

Stockinette Stitch

In the round: Knit every round.

Back and forth: Knit the right-side rows, purl the wrong-side rows.

PROVISIONAL CAST ON

The provisional cast on is an invisible form of casting on. This technique is used when you need to work into the cast-on stitches at a later point in the garment construction, forming an invisible join.

To work, use a piece of smooth scrap yarn and a crochet hook that are both the appropriate size for the yarn you'll be knitting with. Make a chain that contains approximately 10% more stitches than you need to cast on. (For example, if the pattern says to provisionally cast on 50 stitches, make a chain of approximately 55 stitches.) Don't worry if your chain is not perfect; you'll be ripping it out at a later point in the construction of the garment anyway.

Once you have the number of chains required, cut the yarn and pull the tail through to secure; make a knot in the tail so you can identify the end to pull out from later. Now, take a look at your chain. Notice that the front side has "V" shapes on it while the back side has horizontal bars. With the yarn and needles required for the garment, pick up stitches through the bar on the back side of the chain. To do this easily, insert the needle from the top down into the bar, loop the working yarn around the needle, and pull through a stitch. Pick up stitches until you have the required number. Don't worry if you miss a bar along the way. That's why you made the chain longer than you needed!

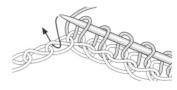

Knit on stitches in the back of the chain.

To remove the chain, simply take out the securing end of the chain (the end of the chain with the knot in it) and place the stitches back on a knitting needle. To assure that the stitches don't get twisted during the process, be sure that the right-hand side of each stitch is toward the front of the needle.

Front of chain after stitches have been picked up

KNITTED CAST ON

The knitted cast on is great when you need to cast on stitches in the middle of a row. It's also useful when you need to cast on a large number of stitches (for an afghan or sweater knit in the round, for example), because you don't have to guess the amount of yarn that will be needed on the tail end of the cast-on yarn. Some people, however, have a tendency to make the knitted cast on too tight, so be careful of this.

Make a slipknot and place it on the needle in your left hand. Go in and knit that slipknot, but do not take it off of either needle. Now, bring the left needle around to the front and pick up the stitch (going from the bottom of the stitch) that was created on the right-hand needle; place it on the left needle.

 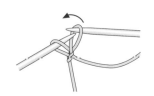

Knit into stitch.   Place new stitch on left needle.

Tighten slightly around needle. Repeat this process, working into the last stitch placed on the left needle, until you reach the required number of stitches.

INCREASES

While there are numerous methods of increasing stitches, the following are the recommended methods for the designs in this book.

Knit in Front and Back of Stitch (K1f&b)

This is one of the most basic and easiest ways to increase. Simply knit into the stitch you want to increase in as you normally would, only don't take the stitch off either needle.

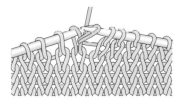

Knit into stitch but do not drop it off left needle.

Bring the right needle around to the back of your work and knit that same stitch again, this time going into the back loop of the stitch.

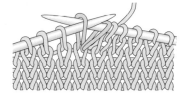

Knit into back of same stitch.

Be aware that this type of increase will result in one normal-looking stitch and one stitch that will have a horizontal bar going across it. You didn't do anything wrong. That is just how this increase looks. Usually this little bar doesn't cause any problems, but on occasion it does take away from the look of the garment, and you may want to opt for a different increase method.

Make One Stitch (M1)

When correctly done, the make-one increase is virtually invisible. Work up to the point where the increase is supposed to go. Pick up the horizontal strand between the stitch just worked and the next stitch by inserting the left needle from front to back and placing the strand on the left needle. Now, knit this stitch through the back loop.

You'll notice that you are actually twisting this stitch as you knit it. If you don't twist the stitch you'll get a hole where the bar was picked up. By knitting into the back of the stitch, you eliminate the hole.

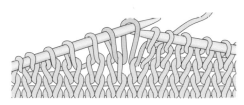

DECREASES

While there are many ways to decrease, the following methods were used for the garments in this book.

Knit Two Stitches Together (K2tog)

This is a right-slanting decrease: when you're done, the stitches will slant toward the right. Instead of knitting the next stitch on the left needle as usual, insert the right needle from left to right through the second stitch and the first stitch on the left-hand needle and knit them as one stitch.

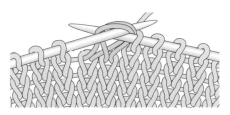

Slip, Slip, Knit (ssk)

This is a left-slanting decrease: when you're done, the stitches slant to the left. It's a mirror image of the knit-two-together decrease. Work up to where the decrease is to be done. Slip the next two stitches individually, as if to knit, onto the right-hand needle.

Insert the left-hand needle into the front part of the stitches, going from top to bottom, and knit these two stitches together, making one stitch out of two.

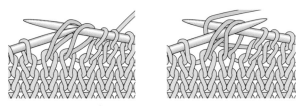

Double Decrease (ddc)

Slip two stitches, at the same time, as if to knit from the left to the right needle. Knit the next stitch. Pass the two slipped stitches (either together or one at a time) over the stitch you just knit and off the needle, making one stitch out of three.

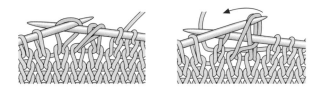

THREE-NEEDLE BIND OFF

This is a very attractive bind off that adds stability to the shoulder area. Place the back shoulder stitches and the front shoulder stitches on separate needles, the same size as you were knitting on. Hold these needles in your left hand with right sides of the knitting together.

Using a third needle (of the same size), knit the first stitch from the front needle together with the first stitch from the back needle, ending up with one stitch on the right-hand needle. Knit the next two stitches together in same manner, ending up with two stitches on the right-hand needle. Now, bring the first stitch you knit up and over the second stitch you knit.

Continue working across the row, knitting one stitch from the front needle together with one stitch from the back needle; every time you have two stitches on the right-hand needle, bind one off. When you get down to one stitch left, cut the yarn, pull the tail through the remaining stitch, and secure.

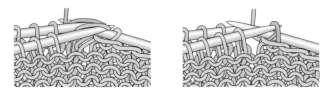

PICKING UP STITCHES

To pick up stitches for the neck band, I find it easier to divide the area where I'm picking up stitches into sections. I also divide the number of stitches I have to pick up and make sure I have them evenly spaced around. For example, if you need to pick up 36 stitches, divide the neck opening into fourths and pick up nine stitches in each section.

To pick up stitches, I find it best to go under both strands of the stitch I am creating the new stitch from. If I go through only the very outside loop, then I'm contorting and pulling the stitch. If I go through both, the stitch stays even and thus there are no holes. Stitches need to be evenly spaced. Since the number of stitches per row is not the same as stitches per inch, you may have to make some adjustments when picking up stitches. You don't need to pick up a stitch in every space across. Just pick them up evenly so you don't have any holes.

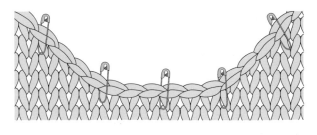

Should a particular stitch appear loose or leave a hole, you can knit this stitch through the back loop and that should take care of it!

I-CORD

I-cord is a wonderful way to make drawstrings and ties for your knitted items. While it may seem a little awkward to do at first, once you get the hang of it, you'll be able to do it in your sleep!

The width of the I-cord is determined by the original number of stitches that you cast on and will vary depending on the weight of yarn you are using. Generally speaking, four stitches is a good number to start with.

Using double-pointed needles in the same size you were using for the body of the sweater (unless the pattern specifies a different size), cast on four stitches. Knit these stitches. *Do not turn the work.* Place the needle with the stitches on back in your left hand and slide the stitches to the opposite end of the needle. Knit these four stitches again, making sure the yarn is pulled snugly behind when brought from the last stitch worked in the previous row to

the first stitch worked in this row. Note that the first stitch you knit in the previous row is also the first stitch you knit in every row. The yarn is pulled across the back each time to start the new row. After three or four rows, you'll notice that you are actually forming a cord.

If your cord is loose, it's most likely because the yarn is not being pulled tightly enough across the back when you begin each row.

Assembly Basics

Use the following techniques to assemble the garment pieces. Feel free to use your favorite techniques if you prefer.

FLAT SEAM ASSEMBLY

This technique is used for sewing the sleeves into the body, as well as sewing seams on booties and mittens.

For shoulders, mark down on both the front and back sections the depth of the sleeve (as given in the beginning of the pattern directions) and place a marker. Now find the center point of the sleeve and place a marker there. Place the right side of the sleeve together with the right side of the body, matching up the shoulder seam with the center-sleeve marker and the sleeve edges with the markers you placed for sleeve depth.

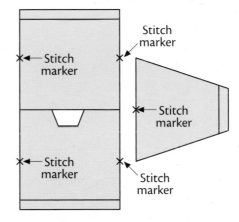

Thread a piece of yarn (or use the tail left from the sleeve bind off if you remembered to leave a long enough one) and sew the pieces together by weaving back and forth. I find it works best when I go through both layers of the bound-off stitch on the sleeve and the outermost loop of the stitch on the body part. This will make a nice, flat seam.

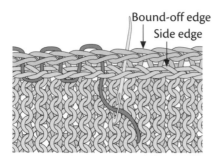

My golden rule is that you must go through each and every bind-off stitch of the sleeve, but you don't have to go through every stitch on the body sections. Simply line up the sleeve section and go through the stitch on the body that is directly across from it. You will find you are skipping an occasional stitch.

For booties and mittens, fold the section to be seamed with right sides together. Weave back and forth under the outside loop of the stitches on each side.

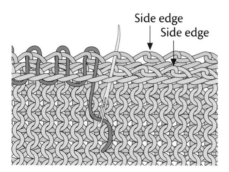

Maintaining an even tension throughout is essential so that your seam doesn't pucker or leave holes.

KITCHENER STITCH

This grafting method is used to join two pieces of knitting together. It's done by creating a row of knitting with a tapestry needle; when done correctly, it's completely flat and invisible.

This method requires live stitches. You'll either have live stitches already on the needles, or you may have to remove a provisional cast on in order to attain live stitches again. The live stitches are then divided equally onto two needles. For instance, if you are grafting shoulders together, the front stitches

go on one needle and the back stitches on a second needle. To graft the top of a sweater hood together (page 48), place half the stitches on one needle and half on a second needle.

Hold the needles together in your left hand, with the wrong sides of the work together and the needle points facing toward the right. Thread a piece of yarn on a tapestry needle long enough to work the number of stitches on the needles. Make sure you have enough yarn so you don't run out partway through.

First Stitch

Front needle: Insert the tapestry needle into the first stitch as if to purl, leave the stitch on the knitting needle, and pull the yarn through.

Back needle: Insert the tapestry needle into the first stitch as if to knit, leave the stitch on the knitting needle, and pull the yarn through.

Remainder of Row to Last Stitch

Front needle: Insert the tapestry needle into the first stitch as if to knit and slip it off onto the tapestry needle. Immediately go through the next stitch on the front needle as if to purl, leaving it on the knitting needle, and pull the yarn through.

Back needle: Insert the tapestry needle into the first stitch as if to purl and slip it off onto the tapestry needle. Immediately go through the next stitch on the back needle as if to knit, leaving it on the knitting needle, and pull the yarn through.

Last Stitch

Front needle: Insert the tapestry needle into the last stitch as if to knit and slip it off.

Back needle: Insert the tapestry needle into the last stitch as if to purl, slip it off, and pull through.

Weave in the yarn tail on the wrong side.

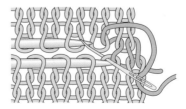

Useful Information

METRIC CONVERSIONS

Yards x .91 = meters

Meters x 1.09 = yards

Grams x .035 = ounces

Ounces x 28.35 – grams

STANDARD YARN-WEIGHT SYSTEM

Yarn-Weight Symbol and Category Names	1 Super Fine	2 Fine	3 Light	4 Medium	5 Bulky	6 Super Bulky
Types of Yarns in Category	Sock, Fingering, Baby	Sport, Baby	DK, Light worsted	Worsted, Afghan, Aran	Chunky, Craft, Rug	Bulky, Roving
Knit Gauge Ranges in Stockinette Stitch to 4"	27 to 32 sts	23 to 26 sts	21 to 24 sts	16 to 20 sts	12 to 15 sts	6 to 11 sts
Recommended Needle in U.S. Size Range	1 to 3	3 to 5	5 to 7	7 to 9	9 to 11	11 and larger
Recommended Needle in Metric Size Range	2.25 to 3.25 mm	3.25 to 3.75 mm	3.75 to 4.5 mm	4.5 to 5.5 mm	5.5 to 8 mm	8 mm and larger

SKILL LEVELS

◼☐☐☐ **Beginner:** Projects for first-time knitters using basic knit and purl stitches; minimal shaping.

◼◼☐☐ **Easy:** Projects using basic stitches, repetitive stitch patterns, and simple color changes; simple shaping and finishing.

◼◼◼☐ **Intermediate:** Projects using a variety of stitches, such as basic cables and lace, simple intarsia, and techniques for double-pointed needles and knitting in the round; midlevel shaping.

◼◼◼◼ **Experienced:** Projects using advanced techniques and stitches, such as short rows, Fair Isle, more intricate intarsia, cables, lace patterns, and numerous color changes.

Resources

The following companies have supplied yarns and/or buttons for this book. Their generosity is greatly appreciated. For a list of shops in your area that carry the products mentioned in this book, please contact these companies.

YARN

Austermann Yarns
Skacel Collection, Inc.
www.skacelknitting.com
Step 6-Ply

Berroco, Inc.
www.berroco.com
Berroco Sox Metallic
Comfort DK

Blackberry Ridge Woolen Mill
www.blackberry-ridge.com
Mer-Made DK Weight

Claudia Hand Painted Yarns
www.claudiaco.com
Fingering 55 Silk
Fingering Weight
Sport Weight

Frog Tree Yarns
www.frogtreeyarns.com
Meriboo

JojoLand Yarns
www.jojoland.com
Rhythm Superwash

Lang Yarns
www.berroco.com
Street

Plymouth Yarn Company Inc.
www.plymouthyarn.com
Dreambaby DK

Sandy's Palette
www.sandyspalette.com
Merino Super DK

Schoeller-Stahl Yarns
www.skacelknitting.com
Fortissima Socka Teddy

BUTTONS

Buttons, Etc.
www.buttonsetc.com

Dill Buttons
www.dill-buttons.com

About the Author

Doreen L. Marquart cannot imagine her life without knitting. She taught herself to knit at the age of nine and has been knitting ever since. Of course, back then she had no idea that her love of knitting would evolve into what it is today. In 1993, Doreen opened Needles 'n Pins Yarn Shoppe, which grew from its small start in a converted one-and-a-half-car garage to a spacious, 1,200-square-foot, custom-built facility that's the largest shop in her area devoted exclusively to the needs of knitters and crocheters!

Doreen earned the title of Master Knitter through the Knitting Guild of America in 1998, Master Canadian Knitter in 2001, and Master Canadian Designer in 2002. She is also a Certified Knitting and Crocheting Instructor through the Yarn Council of America. Doreen's excitement and love of knitting is contagious. She has taught hundreds to knit, ranging from young 4-H members to retired senior citizens. Her enthusiasm inspires her customers and students to challenge themselves and thus achieve things they never thought possible. Her shop has become a refuge and destination stop for knitters of all levels.

Doreen lives with her husband, Gordon, in the unincorporated township of Richmond, located in southeastern Wisconsin. They have three grown sons, Michael, Phillip, and Cody; three daughters-in-law, LeAnn, Katie, and Melissa; and one granddaughter, Addison.

There's More Online!

- Visit www.needlesnpinsyarnshoppe.com to see patterns and kits from Doreen, learn what's new at her shop, and read her blog.

- Check out www.martingale-pub.com to find more great books on knitting, crochet, quilting, and more.

You might also enjoy these other fine titles from

Martingale & Company

Our books are available at bookstores and your favorite craft, fabric, and yarn retailers.
Visit us at www.martingale-pub.com or contact us at:

Martingale®
& COMPANY

America's Best-Loved Craft & Hobby Books®
America's Best-Loved Knitting Books®

1-800-426-3126
International: 1-425-483-3313
Fax: 1-425-486-7596
Email: info@martingale-pub.com